Breaking Bread

Breaking Bread

Poems by

Christine L. Adams

© 2026 Christine L. Adams. All rights reserved.
This material may not be reproduced in any form, published,
reprinted, recorded, performed, broadcast,
rewritten or redistributed without
the explicit permission of Christine L. Adams.
All such actions are strictly prohibited by law.

Cover design by Shay Culligan
Cover image by Luisa Brimble on Unsplash
Olive branch image by Anna Magenta on Unsplash
Author photo by Gene Reed

ISBN: 979-8-90146-919-4
Library of Congress Control Number: 2026938510

Kelsay Books
502 South 1040 East, A-119
American Fork, Utah 84003
Kelsaybooks.com

Acknowledgments

My humble thanks to Dr. Josephine Johnson, W.B. Yeats scholar and former Chair of the Communications Department at the University of Miami, and Todd Young, poet and former New York City teacher of Art and Design, for their careful reading of my manuscript.

As ever, my gratitude overflows for my creative and loving children, Samuel, Elizabeth and Oliver, who offer enthusiastic support for all I do.

Contents

LES DESSERTS

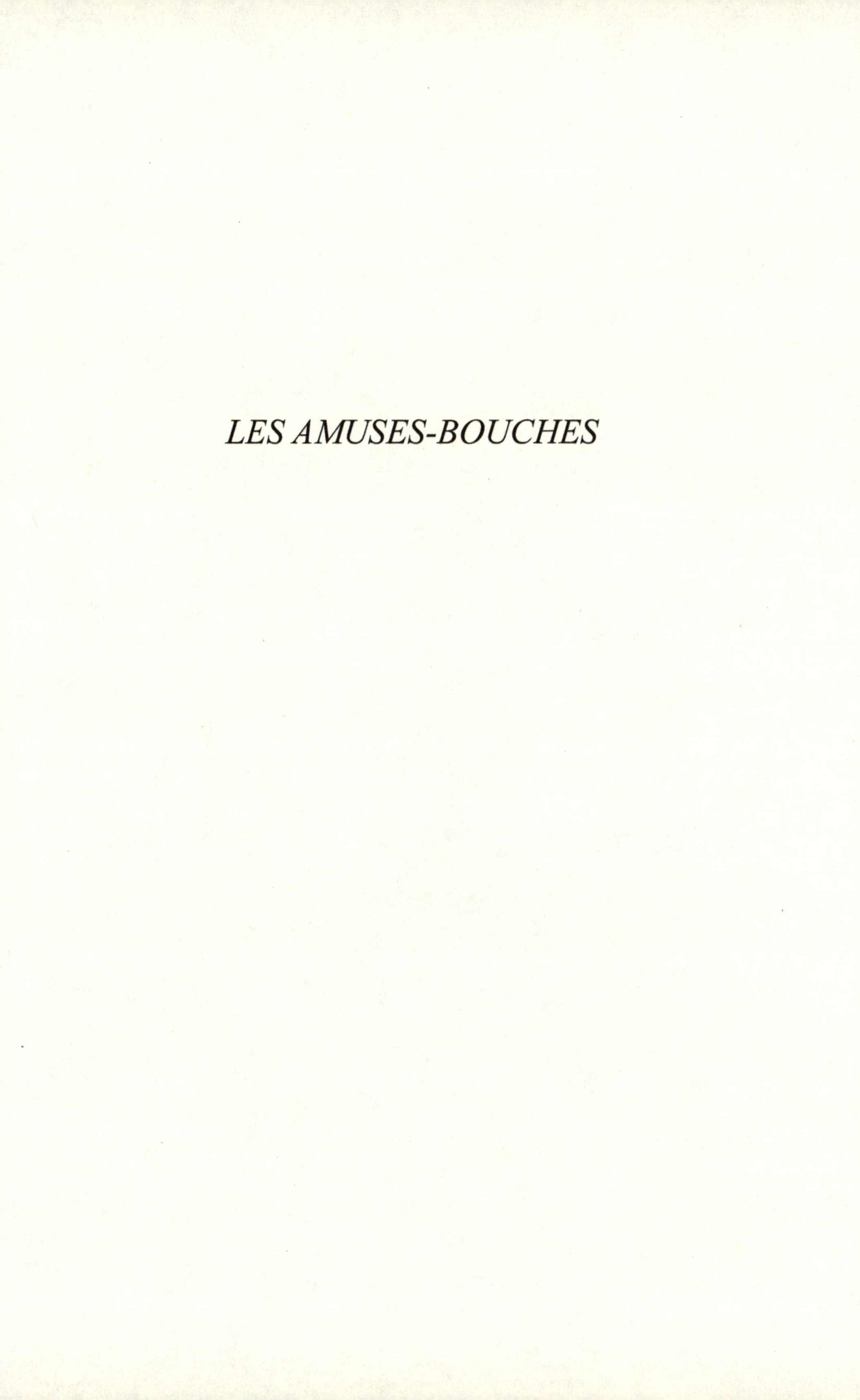

LES AMUSES-BOUCHES

Reveille

The beat, which unruly hearts do break
in obscurity of night, for all time's sake
the moon, who has robbed the day of light
tampers with shapes the eye does take;

thieves and lovers, in obscure dance,
twisting bodies on a blue-beamed trance;
curse the fool, our unruly sun,
arrived through curtains, all askance,

to wash the skin and bathe the eye,
eclipse the dream and quiet a sigh;
for nothing dark is desolation.
Solid rock, in absentia, tried:

guilty of nothing but deflecting light
and mirrors the sun, from great height.

Portrait

Among campily painted portraits
is our photo, taken a few years ago,
a moment, a grain, frozen in
acids, chemicals, a fixer. The phantom
women loom large over us, distorted
somewhat grotesquely and reminiscent
of discomfort in their oils.

I'm not sure if the collection is
a litany of lost desires, remembrances,
or a study of brush strokes, some
folksy, others more sophisticated,
all portraying perfectly smooth skin,
protruding lips and out-of-focus eyes.

There we stand, amongst the
artifice, somewhat true to ourselves.

The grocer told me I hadn't aged a
day in fifteen years this morning,
but I corrected him: I have aged 5,475
of them, some more pleasantly than others.

Some more memorable:
those that were weighted down like
leaden grief, others as light as
sunlit beams of dust;
most passed unnoticed in the
monotony of enduring, marked
by one more cup of coffee, one

more walk to the park with a
canine or another on the end of a leash,
a commute like all the others,
hanging on the end of a strap.

If our portrait was painted, I suppose
it would be a pointillist one, made
of tiny dots, each one marking
the mysterious days we spent
together, apart, engraving
a line on our face, a streak in
our hair, an Archimboldo perhaps,
a composite of every morsel that
sustained us, comforted us,
savored over candlelight
or wolfed down over the sink
as a baby screamed from his crib.

Not a Cindy Sherman, nor a Warhol,
disguised and obscured,
nor a self-portrait, filtered and
self-conscious. A candid!
Truer to a Rembrandt, and honest:
a photomosaic that captures
every moment, a deconstruct.

Because we have aged, and lived, every day;
it's dying we'd prefer to do just once.

Logos

I heard a groom give a speech
on his wedding day, in which
he declared a man wiser than he
outlined the two most important

days in life: the one on which one is born,
the other on the day he learns why.
His dewy-faced bride tilted her head
like a beagle when he professed

she was his why. I bowed my own,
not in reverence, but to contemplate
my own whys, this young man's
ignorant declaration that he had

found the meaning of life, placing
an impossible burden on his beagle
bride. Decades proved to me
that there are many whys.

They aren't static, but shift like
a Tolstoy novel. Life is made of whys
and days you question them, ones
shrouded in grievous challenges.

Their weight can't be borne on
delicate shoulders draped
in white lace, but on ones strengthened
by solitary work and observant eyes.

If I had to choose one “why” it would be the day
I thought I couldn’t but did, reminded by
a flock of merganser ducks who filled a break
in the ice on a New England lake:

small in a large world, working
through the bitter cold, I ignored their annual
appearance until that day, when I understood
that true purpose can only be found

through bridling the pain, and fighting
the elements that hinder us.

Hourglass Figures

"It's my marry 'em and bury 'em
suit," he replied dryly to the earnest
woman seated opposite us. She was
sipping a cold beer from an

amber-colored bottle when his
quip required her to smirk
through her compliment, wrist
to her lips, and cough a reply:

"Well, l'chaim! to that . . ." and
took a more leisurely, feminine
gulp. I looked down at my own
repeat appearance, a black crepe

shift that ably held me during
my own celebrations, and did the
requisite calculations in my head:
thirty years of cocktails, a little snug

for that first postpartum evening out,
loose at the memorial of a life-long
friend whose loss made us all
appreciate that we had time left to

savor this world in slow, savory bites and,
with wisdom, feel joy for our daughters
who complain, naked in front of their closets,
that they haven't a thing to wear.

As You Would Have Liked

This gaudy salon where we feted you
offered a poignant illustration of
the Pigeonhole Principle, where
a subset's cardinality exploded:

those who loved you, or loved us
in your absence. It was an
occasion you would have loved,
your own fête, where every

wall of this fragile birdhouse
shattered, a Hilbert's paradox
of our collective life: where those
that played on each stage

of Jacques' poetical seven ages
gathered together, as only you
would have liked. The only
gathering, solemn and transcendent

where uncomfortable compartments
dissolve. The curtain closes on
your strange and eventful history,
the last scene in which we

observe the main characters in
our own theaters, full of wise saws,
in a world too wide for smallness.
These are the keepers, who notice

that today it isn’t your regular grey
marry ’em and bury ’em suit that you wore,
laid out in celebration, but your dress blues
starched and dignified as you, decorated

with a full bird on your lapel, that we found
in a box in your top dresser drawer.

Ode to the Man Who Filtered My Face on Social Media

He who wants a mule without fault must walk on foot.
—English proverb

A painter with scissors!
A regular Henri Matisse are you,
decoupage with a blinking cursor
and you've resurrected my youth!

Glory! Be the erasures you've
been kind enough to pixilate
all evidence of the lives I've
overcome, won, or better, assimilate!

With a power mightily assigned
to your clicking little mouse,
you've smoothed the tracks
upon my temples and cleaned this earthly house.

With a stroke of an airy brush aligned,
over the grayish orb of each eye,
you chivalrously took my bags, without asking,
and carried them off, with an audible sigh;

Alas, in those bags are frets, *and réveillons,*
a wise lady am I, knowing that I take alight:
that this land has stones, the meat has bones.
So, I'll take it from here, alright?

LES ENTRÉES

The Greek Chorus

There are anonymous
commentators who opine in
our midst. “They”, they are called.
as in, “You know what they say.”
They dispense nuggets of wisdom
with no credentials. No identity,
in fact. Just omniscience in
the face of adversity.
Delivered by various members
of a suburban Thebes,
one might imagine a
chorus of citizens, harmonizing
with lutes. If you listen
carefully, you can hear their projection:
We ignorant mortals! The more we trip
the more we turn to the naughtier
corners of our brain, and still reject
larger shoes for commentary
on another part of the anatomy.

Morsel

Why then, can one desire too much of a good thing?
—William Shakespeare, *As You Like It*

Give it to me in pieces, please,
just a nibble, something easy to stomach,
morsels, a simple, sweet bit, soupçons,
spoonfuls that melt on the tongue like honey,
tidbits, a gobbet, a taste.
Minutiae? It's not trivial. Trifle?
An English dessert, layered in subtle
creams, custards, fruits. Isn't joy
best delivered in snippets? Your cake sweeter
by the bitter coffee that warms my
waking hands? Even those who throw
the grand galas, know
that the angel is in the details.
For bright blue eyes are the most beautiful,
my dear, when gracing a weathered face:
a visage that earned its deepened lines
by squinting into the sun, the same ball
of scorching plasma that blinded us to the
stars, upon which we only see fit
to wish during the darkest of nights.

Fanfare

Aspen trees, symmetrically
growing along an Upstate farm,
catch the mistral-like winds and
wave their leaves like celebratory

sparklers, their silvered, shimmered
undersides catching the light to
twinkle in our dulled eyes, and applaude the
respite from the dry July heat.

Its confetti-like shower is uncannily like
that of the Eiffel Tower, on that nail-
biting first night, when we all
wondered if the world would

end, as we do now, locked down
on our porches looking for ways to
quietly memorialize all that we
neglected, took for granted,

and lost.

Dandy Lion

. . . is how you pronounced
an unwanted plant,
shot through the violet vinca like
a burst of yellow confetti,

its own high-styled
rebel, a wild flower
like you: tenacious,
resilient, hearty,

landed here on the
prevailing winds,
a seed carried
on a child's breath,

without plan or
preconceived notions
on how you were supposed
to be, or to become,

a culinary staple, a
lion's tooth, roaring her
own benevolent yawp
over a Samaritan world.

The Canonization

Science found a way
to carve the essential
from the womb, a surgical
addition to our natural order,
leaving behind a brilliant scar,
proud flesh.
Learned lessons and wisdom
is far sexier, I suppose;
an Arcadian Eden, earthly,
encircled in human arms, is
an ordered mess, an empathic axiom
that jumps on planes,
weeps, kisses wounds,
and answers, as best a mother can.

Original Interrogatory

Answer only the question posed,
offering no additional
information than what was
originally requested:
sage advice from childhood
development specialists.
The first answer will undoubtedly
lead to a second, a third, etcetera,
for the more inquisitive of
tots, until the parent has pieced
together a daisy chain of examples,
a regular Kotex ad of explanations
beginning with "in my uterus" and
ending abruptly with
"sexual intercourse."
The most precocious of them, however,
will push deeper, if you will,
skipping the "Disgustings!" and the
"You did WHAT with Daddy?" and turn
instead to the stickier of subjects.
"But where did the first person
come from?" Blushing, the parent
stumbles over Genesis and Darwin's
hominids, Adam's agnostic
rib, which couldn't possibly have taken
residency in the cage of
Mitochondrial Eve.

Tripping down an endless path made
beautiful by Natural Order,
it's divinity subject to
personal interrogation—
one as endless as the
expanding universe—the
young prodigy shakes her head, disbelieving,
"But I thought she was from Plymouth?"

Faith and Hope

Lefty loosey, righty tighty
I reminded her, under my breath,
as she struggled with the
battery panel to a toy house

built for model people that
looked liked Prozac-laden
versions of ourselves, perma-
grinning, plastic and maniacally

unaffected by the struggle that
ensues at the hands of their
master, their animator, who remains
a few paces ahead of her developing

fine motor skills. The screwdriver shook
and slid from the star-shaped groove
of what should have been second nature, until
the emotional hose of her countenance,

kinked and sharply twisted, violently
burst forth a stream of blood to
her cheeks, tool thrust against the wall,
which needed retouching anyway.

Inhaled through the nose, in one
frustrated stream, exhaled again, with
catharsis, returned to the task at hand:
to illuminate an imaginary world

in electric light, where doorbells
chime a pleasant welcome and all is arranged,
just so.

Newton's Law of Universal Gravitation

Newton's Law of Universal Gravitation
forces an impressionist painting of a river
displayed in our dining room to
hang at a five-degree angle.
Passers-by adjust it, usually with a thumb
and forefinger at one of the lower corners
with delicacy, leaning back on their rear
foot, with a squint and a tilt of the neck
to ascertain the line of the adjacent
window. Alas, the truth of the matter
is the square of the distance of its center
is perfectly equal: it is the house itself,
more than two centuries old, that lists,
to the opposite degree of the art, a mimetic
representation of the river that rushes
by our westerly windows. The structure
is subject to time and its universal effects
on its earthly subjects, shifting sills,
listing beams and turning arthritic joints,
all the while still housing us, embracing us
with silent stoicism, paternal wisdom
and immortal affection.

Chez Nous, II

Not tasted from the
plate set with care
before us, or in a
bottomless cup of

butter tea, bitter
and pungent in its
reality, warm and
encompassing in

concept, an endless
envelope: like music
felt at the base of
the neck, that eases

the strain, taught with
burden, numbers, words
the stark concreteness
of life outside this

place.

Not a brush stroke or
a structure, to dwell,
but a wave of warmth
where the melody

is felt, understood,
the notes left unread.
So pull up a chair.
Stay a while. Stay an

eternity.

LES PLATS

Breaking Bread

The moment they hit the floor, our feet register
the gravity that holds us to
our host, a steadfast challenger
to centrifugal force,

keeping us from being separated from our center
or flung into oblivion: reason enough
to feel gratitude, to adulate
that unseen benefactor

whatever or whomever it may be.
Yet endeavor we must, to bestow
meaning to the endowment without
clear subjugation. So let us begin

here, over this humble loaf, the staff of life,
clear evidence of cultural civilization.
I made it from local flour, seasoned
with kosher salt, yeast, kneaded the dough

with sure hands. The tips of my
fingers as sure of gravity as my
morning toes. I earned every
ingredient of this humble staple,

and saved enough to share another—
with you—to be nourished and adored.

Deconstruction

Say what you mean, but don’t make me
do the work to tear it apart
just to understand what’s under
it all: a language completely uncentered.
Its artificial: a text that can’t
be naturalized or understood,
with or without context, or
empathy or modifications.
It’s a wonder any of us
understand each other, through words
that create tensions; unity
only rises to release some of it.
Modify, edit, add, take away
what you will, yet red will
still be read to me and I will
withhold any meaningless interpretations.
Questions are all any of us has, in truth,
that and the urge to scratch our heads.

The Baby

The Baby, he called it,
his sourdough starter:
the essential ingredient
of his sublime pizza pies,
fired in a wood oven,
constantly attended with a
familial passion that seemed
to transcend what we were eating,
devouring, more like it,
goofily smiling at each other
as if this simple meal was
something more than it appeared
to be,
served in a hole in the wall
with steamy windows, facing
deserted streets of a sleepy
neighborhood. “Don’t eat
it or it’ll be gone,” you said.
It was too perfect to eat,
this meal, culminating a
similarly exalted day, “We’d better
drive carefully on the way
home, as something’s got
to give . . .” Give? More like an offering,
this sacrificial baby with
Neapolitan roots, started and fed
by a doting mother who would
nourish the world, a Columbian

Exchange of her love, her life,
much like the Brazilian votive
left on a Rio altar, in thanks
for a safe delivery: molded in
waxy cultures, a Giza starter,
a Red Sea starter, a sacrificial
lamb, a doughy Isaac, that found its
convoluted way to the table, leaving us
thankful for serendipitous
blessings that are never
as small as they seem

Trompe-l'Œil

Our image, bent and distorted—stuffed
into a convex mirror we purchased
on the Parisian streets of our adopted home—
is a funhouse version of ourselves hung

in a real-world museum, where art
and artifice harkened back to a
grammar school skill: landscape drawing
with a vanishing point, indoctrinating

the youngest students of life to pave
imagined paths to an invisible,
inconceivable possibility. *L'œil de sorcière,*
the eye of the witch, sees us smaller than

we are, a deity's attempt to
relegate us into an oval, molded frame.
We've missed so much obscured in shadows
at our feet, Grace hidden in all that we

ignored at the curb. Truth is a near-sighted
vision, learn what one will,
prepare as one may, for which one feels
grateful rather than blessed. We are not small.

We are here, today, as ourselves,
ignoring regret, hope, and
the objects in the rear view that
are larger than they appear.

Finistère

The end of the earth is
what the French call their
westernmost *département,*
the tip of their beloved ground,

where one can stand at
the edge of a rocky cliff
over rough seas, contemplating
a course to nowhere, the unknown,

with a stone in one's pocket,
heavy, burdensome, worn smooth
with the distal phalanx of the
thumb in painful recollections

and educational regret, or
the converse: a buoy of gratitude
and a truer understanding of
what we share, all of us.

My father described industriousness
as performing a task as if there was
no tomorrow, eagerly, frantically,
without restraint:

As one should wake each day
encountered by the end of the earth,
touching foreheads with a loved one
over a deathbed, clutching hands.

If only such grace existed yesterday
and hindsight be wisdom, we could whisper
thanks and let many tomorrows be the product
of the hard-earned ground underneath us.

Voluntas Vitae

The Magi's gifts are hidden
in the discovery of Everyman's
bequest, a pearl in a shell,
an ability, a benefaction:

the willingness to refine it,
cultured, every shimmery layer
of opalescent nacre, held with
care, simply to be given away

with prudence to a worthy
steward, held indefinitely,
on permanent loan until passed
to another necklace, more precious

than the South Sea's. To be retained by
one, lacking recipient, is to grieve
like a lover with unrequited affections,
like a traveler without destination.

The Network

As evasive as you were, I preferred
to listen to your staccato blurbs
rather than rhetorical, candy-tongued
politicians or priests droning on about

what they think they know, tossing out half-truths
into the blowing winds, feeding the fire.
Disconnected, relegated to our respective
tribes where we belong, we preach

to the choirs of discontent and comfort. It's
as if we've driven into a cell-free zone,
where preservationists question the
health of such things. Words spin

in my car, as I picture you in yours:
self-contained vessels where ideas
are stuck in the throat like the heavy yolk
of an infertile egg one just can't swallow.

Infrastructure

In the last blush of dusk
my son strikes two pieces
of rose quartz, tumbled
to a high unnatural gloss.
Together with successive
clicks, he replicates what
a bohemian docent with
feathered earrings
explained to him:
people of the Ute,
Land of the Sun,
conjured the Spirits of
mid-summer with the
same crystals nestled in
rattles of translucent
buffalo hide.
Glowing internally,
a mechanoluminescent
wisdom, mysterious,
creates encapsulated sparks, as
every neuron, firing dendrite,
axon of his golden body, synapse lit in kind,
forms his Self.
Housed by an ephemeral
pop-up cathedral
of transparent skin,

muscle, blue drops of
aboriginal sanguine fluids,
flow through
a conduit of an
equally black-lit blue,
mixed amongst
ten pints of various,
standard, original
lifeblood.
His own firing light
nurtured by a protective housing,
animates and transports him through space,
allows him to love and fear and despise
privately. House and home
protecting the other,
interdependently,
cooperatively leaving what once
will be known as a footprint,
an impression, a suggestion of
him which will lighten the grey
of the longest systemic shadows
cast from an ivory tower
or ceremonial rattle
with a dull flash.

The Myth of the Morai

Revisionist historians have
nothing on this ninety-nine
million-year-old insect, locked in
Burmese amber, whose
triangular head could
turn 180 degrees—
shattering our own ability
by a full right angle.
The great horned owl,
sagacious-eyed hunter,
evolved, pivots its own
close to a full rotation:
looking back without
repent or regret,
forward with no expectation,
other than the next repast.
No Tolstoy parable could
illustrate the point better,
frozen in natural resin,
no underwriter, no physician.
Let the ink hold fast, for
all we have is now.

Cliché

Careening down a hill, perched on
a scooter, her preferred braking method
a tumbling leap into the grassy median,
my daughter sailed as fast as a cheetah
downhill, finding the brake at last with her foot,
applied while crouching in a ninja position,
her center of gravity low to the ground
until she met with the unforgiving pavement.

We are crouched even lower
to the deck a week later, limping along,
her wound festering white and angry
under the all-important Band-Aid.
I rubbed coconut oil on the adhesive,
the memory of screaming fits on a hospital
bed still vivid, while she stared at
my shaking fingers, the memory gnawing:
she lying vulnerably under a bright light,
my strong arms holding hers in surrender while
she hated me and cursed my betrayal,
swearing she'd never trust me again.
I liken the mother-child relationship
to an arranged marriage, a match
made by Natural Caste, neither choosing the other.
And yet somehow, I fell in love with her
without even knowing her, the idea
of her endearing me, inextricably,

with every movement, every internal
biological sound that I couldn't
decipher from my own. I wonder
if she loved me too, before she was conscious
of what lay beyond that sacred path.
"Rip it off," she said, determined,
knowing full well that somehow I'd
hurt her again, and she me, all the while sharing
the only perdurable love we'd ever know.
With one swift pull, two matching grimaces,
I yanked Rumi's plaster and left the wound
open to the air, to heal, to scar,
to usher in the light our clouded eyes craved.

Wings

My oldest noticed the nest first,
my son who is in love and realizing
what it is to care for another human being,
attached, vulnerable, responsible.

We couldn’t see the eggs, the ball
of twigs and twine out of reach,
but I imagined they were cushioned in dog fur
like the ones of my childhood had been.

The youngest noticed the mother a week later,
feeding worms to sparsely-plumed,
enormous beaks, orange and pleading,
perched atop impossibly thin necks.

The middle, sick of clipped wings herself,
acknowledged the fledglings with boredom,
asking for six points of identification:
birth, security, education, a passport,

when Robin flew off, inciting a tweeting chorus
of conflict: stay! But give us the car keys.

Pandemic

Any man's death diminishes me,
because I am involved in Mankinde.
—John Donne, "Mediation XVII"

Motherhood is a Mary Cassatt painting,
we women are fooled into thinking:
rosy in hue, rounded, warm impressions,
of notions, of natural strength;

yet as soft as any human touch, the
introduction to the world seems as
painful to the newborn child, who
howls like an animal in the new

cold light, hitting his coated skin
like a shock wave of truth, stinging
his senses once easily lulled to
sleep in a warm amniotic bath.

My experienced sister told me, as I nested in place:
consider the first three months of a child's life
a personal emergency. Keeping him alive
will require one's personal liberties to be

stripped as convicted, to return later in
glorified pieces that merely resemble what
we once knew. What I once knew was
a lost woman who trod a path she thought

was clear; I mourned her, buried her, tipped a hat
to one who now understood her purpose,
in her milky quarantine. Life was not her own,
nor was it ever. For mankind, we begin again,

one body at a time, a collective. The infant in arms,
in a nursery, where frost on a pre-dawn window
blooms a silver bouquet, spreading its cold
branches illuminated in moonlight,

cradled, one of many new beginnings,
his skin flushed pink where it touched mine.

Primordial Dust

A pile of shoes lay by the door,
on the threshold of public and private life,
kicked off to keep the floors of the
temple passably clean.

There are well-worn tennis shoes,
for motherly duties,
Pumps with a sensible kitten heel, in
which a woman could tip-toe over the

broken glass of a still male-dominated
world. Cycling clips and
running sneakers to keep the body
working well, more finely tuned,

sandals for days when shoes
are required but too hot to bear.
All had embedded in their soles
small pieces of the ground they

covered, some well, some
more softly trod.
These tiny pieces of earth, kept
and carried to this:

the place one presently belongs,
a temporary dwelling, that is
merely made a home, so long
as one can carry invisible reminders

from where we have come, the
primordial dust, and all the forever
homes we have left behind.

Isometric Exercise

Plank, a stiff board, the base,
a floor, fundamental to the aim:
in this case, core strength,
invisible to an observer

who can't see the muscle
fibers straining to keep
the body afloat, light as
a feather, stiff as a board.

The work is static:
no movement, no joints
swinging like hinges. A
stabilizing, internal spar

between a planner's desire
for the robust ability for
fight, for flight and the
instinct to lie down in a heap.

Marcus Aurelius spoke of
joyful presence; the stoic,
of gratitude; Buddha, of
living in the moment;

Horace, to seize the day, aye,
one must stand mindfully still to run,
hidden preparedness ticking
like intricate clockwork.

First Person Narrative

Seem, feel, look, taste,
sound, appear, become:
verbs of being, a personal
reality, whereby red is not

scarlet, amaranth, carmine
or falu; but a stitched letter
of public shame, a rose,
a stain on the lips or

the façade of a New England
barn. Living is largely a
solitary, hopeful,
human affair, whereby

perception is dominated
by bleeding colors.
Fearing no god, vulnerably,
one blazes a unique path

in search of another
with a similarly mysterious
sensory process, who sanguinely
has none of the answers.

Mrs. Kinzler

A Pittsburgh housewife is credited
for flying the American flag
on the moon, where gravity grounds nothing
and the atmosphere hosts myth.

A womanly contribution to the Apollo
missions, at an inhospitable time for Her:
a curtain rod pocket and a pole to
pierce the lunar visage,

made of paper, cheese, igneous
rock, depending on one's own celestial
mood, literary knowledge
or state of rational being.

Imagine the man on the moon
staking claims, driving golf balls
or longing towards a blue-green
orb at an impossible distance,

sliding down his own beams,
inquiring the way to Norwich, or
my lonely arms, finding nothing but
cold porridge that somehow burned his lips.

Preferring ethereal surroundings of weightlessness
dangling over paper seas, he pulls her waters and
synchronizes the cycles of every terrestrial womb,
crowding delivery rooms on the brightest nights.

He remains an unrequited love
evasive during the darkest hours
and brilliant on the last ones when the
light that is reflected is—in sooth—our own.

Relay

Nothing that is worth doing can be achieved in our lifetime; therefore we must be saved by hope.

—Reinhold Niebuhr

I could fill Volumes with Descriptions of Temples and Palaces, Paintings, Sculptures, Tapestry, Porcelaine, &c. &c. &c.—if I could have time. But I could not do this without neglecting my duty. The Science of Government it is my Duty to study, more than all other Studies Sciences: the Art of Legislation and Administration and Negotiation, ought to take Place, indeed to exclude in a manner all other Arts. I must study Politicks and War that my sons may have liberty to study Painting and Poetry Mathematicks and Philosophy. My sons ought to study Mathematicks and Philosophy, Geography, natural History, Naval Architecture, navigation, Commerce and Agriculture, in order to give their Children a right to study Painting, Poetry, Musick, Architecture, Statuary, Tapestry and Porcelaine.

—John Adams to Abigail Adams, 12 May 1780

A starter's gun sees fit to startle runners
into swift mobility: igniting the quadriceps
in twitches, locked in the blocks, to
more productive action.
Metal spikes imbedded into the soles of athletic
shoe, connecting with a gravel track,
reverberate in the jaw, the teeth, grinding
like an un-oiled gear, propelling
the body forward.
A hollow painted aluminum baton
whistles a beat, a bitonal melody,
a rhythm matched by the maker,
by movement and puffs of air.

Knuckles locked closed, gripping a weight,
requiring a give, a take,
compensation for a body
off balance. With weakened back,
the crop is sown in a farmer's field,
untilled and black with richness
and possibility.
Second leg, a political war
of kinesthetics,
the warrior recognizes space, time
opponents in the arc of a goal.
Baton! He yells, and raises
a blue-veined forearm:
a battle cry.
For a fraction of a second,
contact is made, hand to stick to hand,
brotherly, unified, rising into striding sync:
a mathematician calculates
forward progression.
Precision in the final laps,
A philosopher whirring wheels
breaks a tape with powerful pectorals
inflated with steady inhalations—
unbated—unified in hope
of the three cyclic lifetimes
that ran before him, churning
the cinder of an ignorant path
beneath his spent feet.

Winter Solstice

Omnipresent,
this injured child, propped
on her hip, arm looped
around her waist, hand palmed
at the half moon crescent of her
buttock, pelvic bone locked
in her cramped fingers.
The child, the mother, the woman:
bound, each to each,
bedraggled, malnourished,
chaffed and tattered, less like
Jacob's chains, more like
a braided scar that
was healing tenderly,
sensitively numb to touch.
Behold what makes
her heart leap, for one:
migrating mergansers,
whose crests, disheveled
from diving to great depths,
arrive on a cold New England Lake,
on the darkest day of the year.

Rites of Passage

Snow fell in gentle waves
caressing the banks of a river,
singing a lullaby in steady whispers
over a harnessing, ancient dam.

Inclement warmth and winter rains
melt the icy duvet that draped native
mountain laurel surrounding a lake
that knows only one outlet—

this channel that ushers frantic waters
to a welcoming place where
there is room to spread their
anxious liquid wings:

an ocean, limitless, starting at its delta,
its alpha, providing sovereignty, possibility,
the warmth of suns that raise weightless clouds
which will guide our waters home, again.

Loft Living

True Colonials are chopped, cornered,
center-chimneyed, with puritanical walls
creating charming nooks in which to
hide, with antiquated mechanisms.

We preferred loft living, a space
without the cordoned compartments, open:
where moon-faced children,
reflecting light, can hear

our shared soundtrack, a Joy
of Man's Desiring. Clutching
fistfuls of color, they'll
recognize me as I stumble

over their boots left in a
row by the glass-paned door,
as I peel root vegetables, and
sweeten them with dried herbs

which will sustain us through
this savory New England winter.

Defiance in Ohio

An audacious act it is, to fly,
dangling where we don't belong
as homo sapiens. We have evolved
to ambulate, foot to earth, grounded;

and yet a set of brothers, Ohioans no less!
took the writings of a French ornithologist
a leap too far, loved Leonardo a touch too
deeply, allowing themselves to be seduced

by the decidedly erotic vocabulary
of flight physics. Presumably Orville
hatched at birth, imprinted on an eagle,
a hollow-boned soarer, as if it really

was possible to fly. It's unnatural, Wilbur.
We don't belong up here contemplating
the winds, decisions, turns, and shifts,
the entire course of our personal history,

plucking the petals of one daisy, singular in
the chain, that brought us happily to this gate.

Ode to the Brassière

At the turn of the century came you,
freeing our confined corseted torsos
from high fashion, short-sighted spleen crushers,
little more than whale-boned straight jackets

that deformed our skeletal frames and
reoriented our internal organs to keep
us swooning with an idealized
twenty-two inch waist.

Grâce à vous, le soutien gorge,
patriarchal control would shift
from our now-free-breathing
stomachs to our boosted racks,

enticingly framing our throats
with pudgy half orbs, a *décolletage*
to frame our newly-oxygenated cheeks,
our pink visage.

Rocketed, coned, useless pockets
in various colors and fabrics, we breasts
rose in praise, pointing to the sun
we longed to feel with our virginal skins.

Yet you singed in protest
engulfed in flames ignited by
angry love-hungry hippies,
and rose from the ashes

like a wispy phoenix in the form
of the bralette, barely there
slips of cloth left best to the
flatter-chested of girls to fly

with first amendment sensibilities
in the face of misogyny.
Decades later, under a glass ceiling,
you held our milk-engorged bleeders,

protected under layers of absorbent cotton
in conference rooms populated
by gawking men.
Exhausted under silk, sexually confusing

for all present, and loudly hinting
to the more sentient amongst us:
the only real purpose of these gorgeous mounds
is to fulfill their true desire,

to simply do what the powers
of natural order expect of them:
to feed a hungry world.

Dominion

A true dilemma exists for this conflicted hound
in a world beyond his stove-warmed paws:
to follow his nose, to thee, unbound!

Our joints ache while the storm rages on,
forced to sing in domestic round, yet
a singular dilemma exists for this conflicted hound.

Soup simmers in a drafty house, the radio murmurs
of life in milder climes: where he might
follow his nose, to thee, unbound?

To sleep, once more, after injected pause
welcomed first for novelty, a break from the norm
he dreams of a dilemma, this conflicted hound.

To wake, once more, squinting in the sun
tethered and tripping through drifts of snow, he'd prefer
to follow his nose, unbound.

Strains for freedom, tugs at the leash
reminding sore shoulders of old injury
a true dilemma exists for the conflicted hound
to follow his nose, or to thee, be bound.

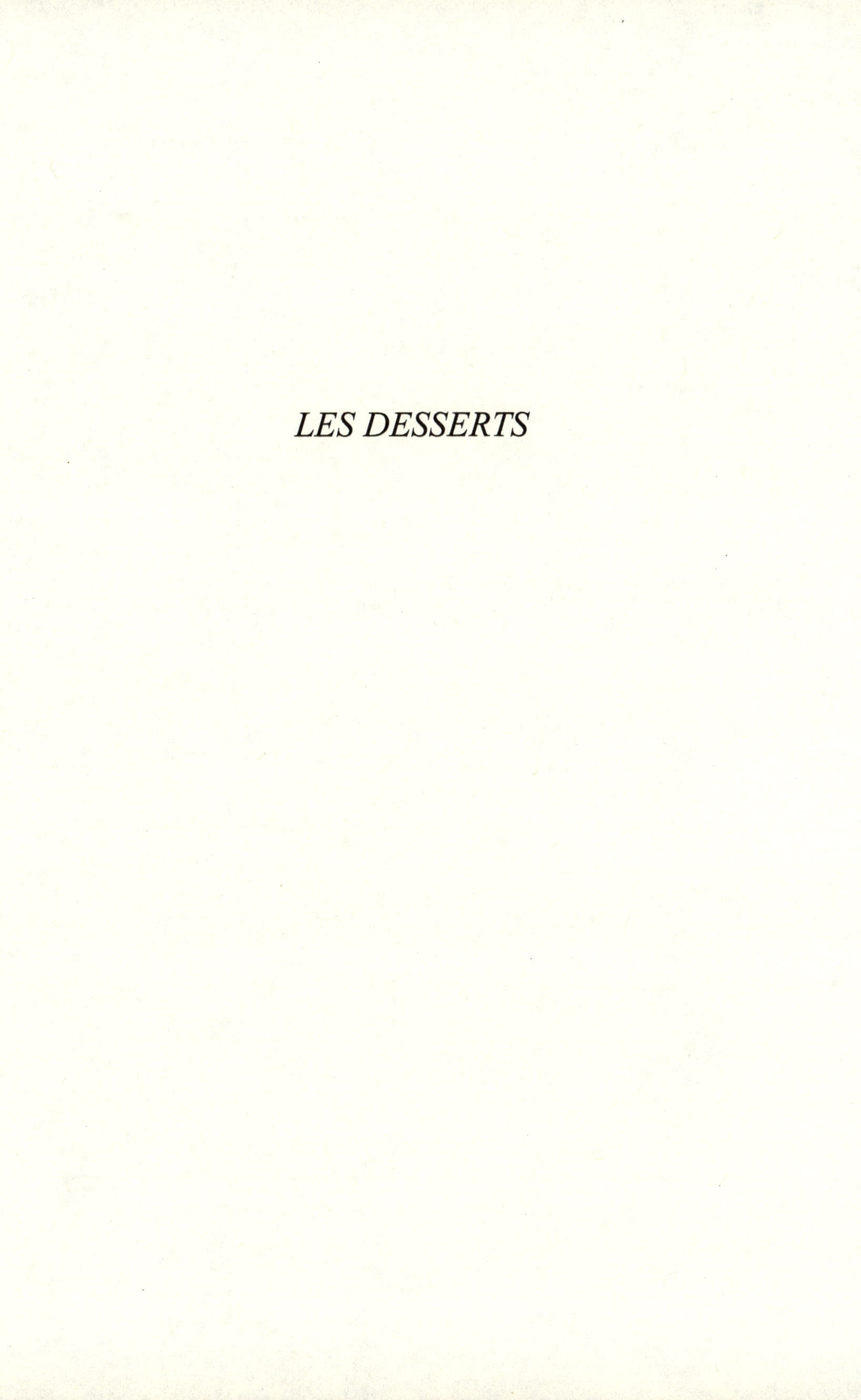

LES DESSERTS

Archimedes' Principle

Ignore the laws of physics for
they don't apply to chemistry.
Try as one will, but that
stiff upper lip will crack.

The weight of heavy matter
will remove to the bottom.
Just let them lie. Read them
like prophetic tea leaves.

They tell a mere fable as
fictional as revisionist history.
Learn the lesson, and proceed to
today, when the Southern sun

warms the hardened face and
boiling water bubbles to the top.

Something Sweet Upon Learning of My Lover's Indiscretion with an Airline Attendant

It has been weeks since
you hung this gaudy
capsized bottle,
adorned with red
plastic flowers, on
our porch, designed
to attract hummingbirds by its
manufactured engineering.

You filled the glass with a simple
solution of water,
a substance so soft
it can cut stone, and
sugar, simple, sweet, essential
and balanced in the bloodstreams
of every living organism.

You share no blood
with my daughter
with whom you hung this
ridiculous thing, you are
no relation, other than human
your pained hearts pump
DNA that is incompatible,

yet curiously in rhythm,
at times, as they free themselves
from anxious restraints.

Here on my porch there are
no gifts from the universe,
no restored faith in humanity.
just a graceful gesture
in the middle of mayhem.

It is a quiet morning on
which they arrive, beating
their wings at an incomprehensible
speed, tiny visions, fairies,
a beautiful reveal of a
vulnerable ruby throat
to delight, to love
my own mischievous Puck
in your absence.

Memorial Day

Dusk extinguished the day,
its wicks of pink ignited clouds
burned to carbonic cords
of grey, while the birds quieted

their melody leaving the
percussion to the peepers,
the hyla crucifer,
to dismiss the band, and

call to other cross-bearing
frogs, a love song to their betrothed
from greater than six feet.
The female will lay her eggs,

after a socially intimate
rendezvous-vous, in a near-by pond
on an antique farm, while we mourn
the dead of our wars, avoidable,

those fighting a virus, perhaps
not as avoidable, and
slug the dregs of what's left
of the rose-colored wine.

We long to embrace our guests,
two kisses on the cheek goodnight,
bid adieu; but instead, we
retreat to our homes to join,

at leisure, from across state lines,
those incessant, blessed frogs.

New England Mille-Feuille

You are the oak tree that
incorporated the entirety
of a bicycle into your trunk,
an oddity of your growth
habits, to encompass the bike
left behind by a child who
no longer wanted it. Your
bark, spilling over the
rusted crossbar like a
primordial ooze,
viscous and precariously
supportive, until the
ultimate, Shel Silverstein
sacrifice left you an
obliging stump, revealing
the rings of your past:
widely spaced and pink
at the center, scarred by
draught, fire, trauma at
the radial lines, which you
carried with a steadfast
stoicism. You threw your
acorns to the forest floor,
rich in decomposing foliage.

There is no closure, only
nurture, taking what you have
learned to bear fruit, the caps of
which made shrill whistles
for children, reminding the world
of their undeveloped presence, shaded
by a collective canopy. No, you will never
be the Charter Oak, boastful, old,
rubbing knotted elbows with
King Charles, pompously
granting unprecedented autonomy
to the State of Connecticut.
Your wood will never comprise
the governor's desk; but we will
look to you, noble savage, and
patiently await your counsel;
when your leaves are the size
of a mouses's ear, we will plant corn,
we will feed even the ungrateful children,
we will nourish the world.

If Not for You

The dashboard gasped 98 degrees
while Bob Dylan whined that he couldn't
even find the floor without me, when
I kissed the bumper of a tall

stranger from West Orange, New Jersey
who looked nothing like the brooder from
Duluth, Minnesota, but a grumpy
pavement dweller, whose eyebrows

separated when I chuckled a
cordial greeting, offered my insurance
card, made small talk about the poorly
designed parking lot at Kings Market,

which somehow brought us, via the amount
of miles on my relatively new
car, to the Boulders Inn, still
operational in 1986,

where perhaps I prepared his smoked trout
mousse, a warmed beet salad for his wife,
enriching her blood to prepare for their
son, conceived that evening. A police

report ushered the end to our second
bump and closed another circle, when
I wished his family well, rolled down
the windows, silenced Bob while the two

distinctly arched eyebrows, framed in pavement,
directed me from the corner in
which I had found myself. It was then
that he thanked me for the warmed beet salad.

Doorknob Artistry

I think it happened when I wiped away
the hidden messages my daughter
left me on the bathroom mirror, and again when
sepia-stained images of my long-gone people

left darkened rectangles on the wall,
where the sun couldn't reach. Again, it struck
with a linen duster I bought
20 years earlier in a flea market,

tucked into a big blue IKEA sack used to masquerade
Labrador retrievers riding the subway, another,
on a mattress that I shared with my own arthritic hound,
carted away by a man who said, "You saved me."

The mysterious noises from my
teenagers' rooms have grown silent,
bottles of wine turned to
vinegar and poured down the drain.

The pile of shoes at the back door
replaced by a trash bag of
wrappers and mismatched socks, matchbooks
with no strikers, disposable wooden chopsticks.

Broken dishes. A Puzzle piece
of Mona Lisa's curved lower lip,
mysterious pieces of plastic.
The Bluetooth speaker amplifies Dylan,

who stayed in Mississippi a day too long,
humming neither justice nor rhyme, while
shedding what doesn't serve in this
house, a home, no longer mine.

Ode to the To Do List

> *The list is the origin of culture. It's part of the history of art and literature. What does culture want? To make infinity comprehensible. It also wants to create order.*
>
> —Umberto Eco

Bullet-pointed, hash-marked,
numbered, prioritized or collected
in order of cognitive
awareness, combating

with each senior moment: a Sisyphean
conquest to close any black hole
of tasks, curiously
recorded for the ages.

We praise thee, oh words
as powerful as the proverbial pen
scribbling persuasive arguments
via epistolary quest,

a Dear John to forgetfulness,
an appeal, a refund of insanity
for thinly veiled organization.
Let this inventory of tasks

restore our autonomy,
our powers of control,
fool us into thinking
with each catalogue of chores

every enumeration of jobs:
we've got it all under
our ink-stained thumbs.
As we tick a check mark

to the margin of our registers,
or more violently
scratch out lines with
frantic blistered fingers, clutching a #2 pencil,

let us slice pieces of
our laden worlds away
with a sharpened nib
and cut away the cancers

of our lives with
every tiny accomplishment.

Sedum

Hardy, succulent leaves
begin to appear when Frost
is musing over a fickle yellow,
and the winter still has its

talons sunk into its prey,
the earth, frozen in wait
for the celebration that is tucked
between the equinoxes.

She mused that she didn't
know the correct names
of any plant, as her earthy
grandmother had taught her

the vernacular; *Live Forever*
is what sedum's Autumn
Joy was called in the Maritimes,
and every flower was a posey.

She assigned the same
name to every granddaughter:
Simplifying them all to a collective:
Susie Q, even the one that

was her namesake. Every sheepdog
was Charlie; every chihuahua,
Marta, a mother figure who would
take immortal shape, a rising

moon, forever waxing, whose
touch was enduring as Love.

Towing Caution in the Wind

Brothers in the boat declared
one must commit to the turn,
cut it, rip it open, and ignore your
instincts. If you ever really

want to be any good, you
have to be scared and do it anyway.
Heed-able advice from two bags of
injuries, fools, who were

damned content
in this second-hand vessel.
I used dish soap to pull the
stiff binding around a lumpy

Achilles' tendon, jumped in,
grabbed the rope, and heard
No Sunday drags here. No
Bullshit. Time's a-waistin'.

So I succeeded.
And I failed. Under the water,
everything was quieter, and
tinted green, the sound

of the motor oddly distant
and tinny, light rippling
and bending with the water
a bit of my blood. Baptized,

breaking the surface, a brother
yelled, Yeah, baby! As I cried
Uncle, crawled into the boat
like an exhausted amphibious

victor. Did you feel it, baby?
No one gets to call me baby,
I said, and though as certain as taxes,
I felt it. A delightful pain.

Stop being such a girl, said a brother,
winked, threw a towel at me
that had warmed dry in the sun,
and cooed, It'll be OK,

Baby.

Come Again

. . . painted on a piece of pine, perched atop
your double-hung sash, is a vintage sign
with shaded letters, "hello" on the opposite
side. An antique is something older,

seventy-five years or more, yet a
generation is a mere thirty. I had a great uncle
who used the phrase as a request, cupping his
hand behind his ear, squinting both eyes,

he'd shout, "Come again, young lady . . .?"
which would make my sisters giggle and
cover their own mouths. We'd repeat what
we had just said, in a shout, trying to keep

a straight face, as I do so today, overwhelmed
with content. We have returned to this place
we knew so well, finding it hard, still,
not to giggle, to ignore the innuendo,

the triple entendre of joy, of grabbing
a hold of what was lost, now, for good.

An Homage to Sir Andrew Augecheek

FOOL
Would you rather hear a love song or a song about the good life?

SIR TOBY BELCH
A love song, a love song.

SIR ANDREW
Ay, ay. I care not for good life.

Feeling sated by a shared meal and a rare
fellowship for a family far-flung with
grown-up lives hindering us, we fall back
into an unspoken line, re-creating

a long-lost dynamic in the name of
nostalgia, of yearning, behaving more
like school children than those burdened
with keeping the lights on, the beds made.

We share stories of the day, now with
the high-tech aide of pocket computers
we all have to chain us to our responsibilities,
Show-And-Tell with digital photography,

the short leash held in our trembling hands. My daughter
shares a video of a raccoon, given pieces of cotton candy
which disappear in a puddle where he washes
his full paws, waving his tiny human-like

digits through the artificially sweetened water,
gazing at the camera through a forlorn mask.
My youngest daughter—virginal—weeps at the cruelty.
Silence greets her, interrupted by laughter as the wise

amongst us recall the lost moments of our own
desires, love scorned, gripping onto beautiful
illusions, tantalizing images as ephemeral as
puffs of smoke, vapor trails, or digital messages.

A grievous moment, when one realizes they are
holding nothing, counterintuitively making the release
more vigorous, a lamenting handicraft echoing that of
Sir Andrew, our recognized Shakespearean fool:

the comic sadness of spun sugar, which dissolves
so quickly on the tongue, albeit adored once too,
as some ancient ancestor summons a brogue in my throat,
not my own, to sing with a sobering hilarity:

*A stick in me hand and a drop in me eye,A doleful damsel I
heard cry, Johnny Blue, we hardly knew ye . . .*

Antecedent

A katydid chirped
somewhere in this
200-year-old cottage,
interrupting the nightly
rituals, the scramble to
finish everything on the
proverbial fifteen-year-old plate.
A lightning rod for all teenaged
concerns diverted anxiety onto
one undeserving creature
that has but one year to live
himself.
She is less entomophobic, more
stuck in the middle of
push and pull, making the
daily decision to provide, need, or
want, to place her hands on the
end of the rope that is manned by the
appropriate team.
This time, her younger self wins:
not the one who complains about
the sensitivity of her navel,
the grimace of the ancient place
that once connected her to her host; or
feels annoyance by
the dichotomy of responsibilities
of the child/parent who diverts trips home
through her ancestral village
to flip switches that her own
octogenarian mother can't reach,

but the one who revels in the
foregone conclusion that
her mother will always want
to cradle her in the palms of
her warm hands, the same ones
that transport a green grasshopper
to a more obliging, al fresco
surrounding.
Sleep comes, tucked into
a familiar fetal position,
at the end of the day when she reflects
on all that has become ours, the
lists, the burden of what she carried, but ultimately,
under the pacific weight of a quilt that allows
respite, and a feral understanding
of the comfort it is to live where we belong,
to be essential, at both ends of the rope.

The Baptism

Voices, indiscriminate, mingled with
the rushing water, white noise
suggestions of unfinished conversations,
whispered and bellowed
during this interminable day.
If I closed my eyes I could
conjure the river in the Spring:
unfiltered melted snow rushing
next to an old Indian trail
long since paved over,
lavender on its banks, the oil
of which perfumes a colicky baby's bath.
Wash away the day, you say,
crawl into bed with no hint
of the dust that sticks
to your skin, that burdensome layer
sent to the waterways with
the race of men who live
in its rapids.
The nights should pass as fast
as years with young children.
Slow the day and walk on the earth with dry feet
sound, *circum caput,* no longer
plagued like Macbeth, but
reborn, unburdened, present
and able to rest.

Berceuse à la Une

Thinking night thoughts, lying supine,
hearing echos of the why's and how's
one sings an oxymoronic opus
of deafening silence,

in itself a sharp fool, an etymological
contradiction in terms that
seems to fit the syntactic bill:
we sophomoric emotional wanderers

make music between the notes,
a tinnitus nocturne punctuated
by pizzicato plucks of a string
of a staff, holding an ephemeral,

Venetian shadow song of memory.
return to a rubato, diminuendo,
a solo, one's own composition:
whole and melodic.

Penultimate Euphemism

When the Sonne Shinto
Make Hay, Whiche is to Say,
Take Time When time
Cometh, lest time steale
Away.
—John Heywood, *A Dialogue Conteinyng*
the Number in Effect of all the Proverbs
in the English Tongue, 1546

We're burning daylight here,
when we should be making hay.
Why linger, lolly gag, dilly dally
dwindle, piddle, procrastinate
twiddle thumbs or amble along,
tarry away, while away,
take our sweet time while it burns?
We're only here for a short visit,
anyway, and opportunity
is knocking loudly on the door,
behind which the fat lady
is warming up, trilling her
scales, which are at a
tipping point.
Can't fritter away, vegetate,
cogitate, kill time, horse around
on this boondoggle; time is ticking,
but that is that. It's curtains for all
of us, a done deal. The checkered
flag is waving. We've saved up to
buy the farm, a one-way ticket,
biting the dust on a permanent
vacation. Elvis just left the building,

dropped the mic, and
is kicking a can, or a bucket
to meet his maker and take a long
nap with the fishes. He cashed in
his winnings, and is growing daisies
now, retired. It's past sunset.
We're not ready to ring down the curtain,
or join the choir invisible;
we haven't come to Jesus, on the other side.
Alas, just as sure as taxes,
we're doing it,
and as we only have one,
we might as well
get down to it.

About the Author

Christine Adams, author of *Setting the Table in the Age of Reason* (2024), has creative work appear in *Litchfield Magazine, The Red Wheelbarrow, Connecticut Magazine,* and connecticuthistory.org, among others.

A grant writer and not-for-profit professional, she celebrates the connective beauty of nature and historic places and is active in the preservation and conservation movements in her historic town. The mother of three, she lives in an 18th-century mill in Washington, Connecticut with her beagle, Rosie.

www.ingramcontent.com/pod-product-compliance
Lightning Source LLC
LaVergne TN
LVHW090532110826
845146LV00003B/1071

* 9 7 9 8 9 0 1 4 6 9 1 9 4 *